THE BEATLES
FOR AUTOHARP

ISBN 978-1-4584-0762-7

HAL•LEONARD®
CORPORATION
7777 W. BLUEMOUND RD. P.O. BOX 13819 MILWAUKEE, WI 53213

Visit Hal Leonard Online at
www.halleonard.com

CONTENTS

The Ballad of John and Yoko

Words and Music by John Lennon and Paul McCartney

Intro
Verse

Moderately fast ♩ = 135

1. Stand-in' in the dock at South Hamp-
2. Fin-'ly made the plane in-to Par-
   Par-is to the Am-ster-dam Hil-

-ton,   tryin' to get to Hol-land or France. _
-is,   hon-ey-moon-in' down by the Seine. _
-ton,   talk-in' in our beds for a week. _

_____ The man in the mac _____ said, _____ "You've
_____ Pe-ter Brown _____ called to say, _____ "You can
_____ The news-peo-ple said, _____ "Say, what-

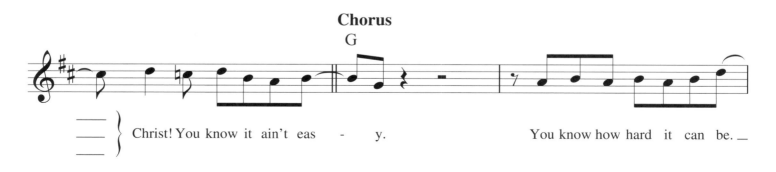

got-ta go back." You know they did-n't e-ven give us a chance. _
make it O. K., you can get mar-ried in Gib-ral-tar near Spain." _
cha do-in' in bed?" I said, "We're on-ly tryin' to get us some peace." _

Chorus
G

_____ } Christ! You know it ain't eas - y.   You know how hard it can be. _

The way things are go - in', ____

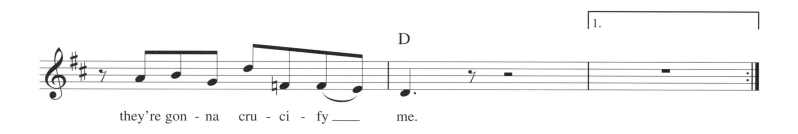

1.

they're gon - na cru - ci - fy ____ me.

2.   3.   **Bridge**
                   G

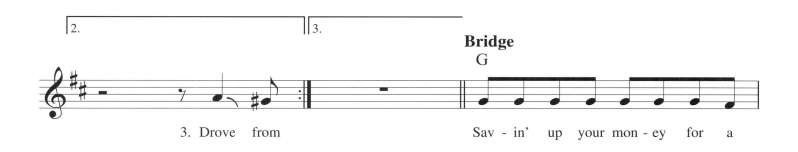

3. Drove from   Sav - in' up your mon - ey for a

rain - y day, ____   giv - in' all your clothes to char - i - ty.

A7

Last night the wife said,   "Oh boy, when you're dead you don't take noth - in' with you but your

Verse
N.C.   D

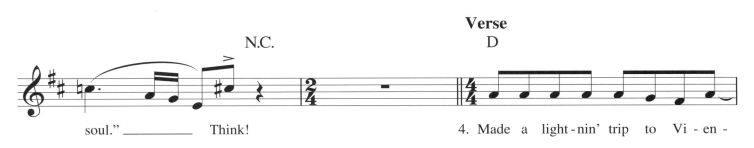

soul." _____ Think!   4. Made a light - nin' trip to Vi - en -

-na, eat-ing choc'-late cake in a bag. ____ The

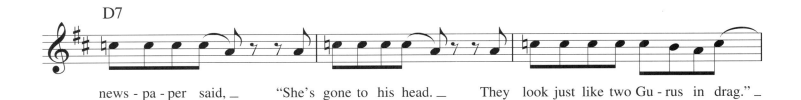

D7

news-pa-per said, _ "She's gone to his head. _ They look just like two Gu-rus in drag." _

Chorus

G

____ Christ! You know it ain't eas - y. You know how hard it can be. _

D   A7

_____ The way things are go - in' _____

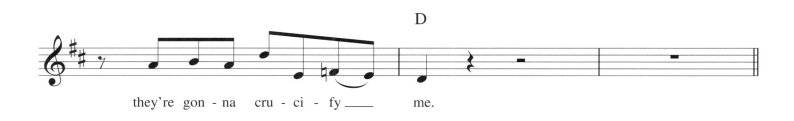

D

they're gon-na cru-ci-fy ____ me.

Verse

D

5. Caught the ear-ly plane back from Lon-don, fif-ty a-corns tied in a sack. _

D7

The men from the press _ said, "We wish you suc - cess. _ It's

Chorus
G

good to have the both of you back." Christ! You know it ain't eas - y.

D

You know how hard it can be. _____ The way things are go -

A7   D

- in' ____ they're gon - na cru - ci - fy ____ me.

A7

The way things are go - in' _____

D

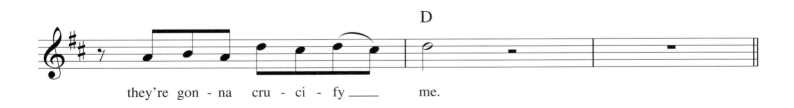

they're gon - na cru - ci - fy ____ me.

Outro
A7   D

Day Tripper

Words and Music by John Lennon and Paul McCartney

Intro
Moderately fast ♩ = 138

𝄋 Verse

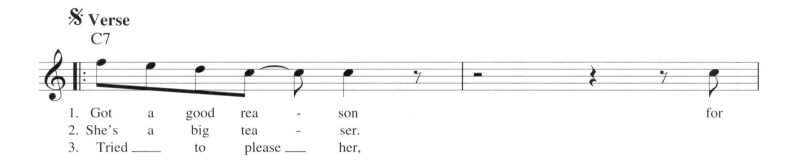

1. Got a good rea - son
2. She's a big tea - ser.
3. Tried ___ to please ___ her,

tak - ing the eas - y way out. ___
She took me half ___ the way there. ___
she on - ly played ___ one night stands. ___

Got a good rea - son
She's a big tea - ser.
Tried ___ to please ___ her,

Chorus

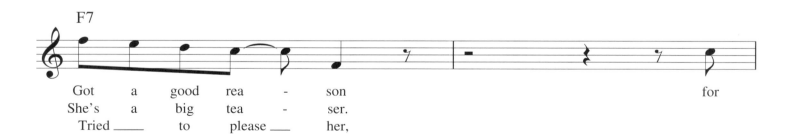

tak - ing the eas - y way out, ___ now.
She took me half ___ the way there, ___ now.
she on - ly played one night stands, ___ now.

She was a day ___

To Coda ⊕

one way   tick - et,   yeah. __
one way   tick - et,   yeah. __
Sun - day   driv - er,   yeah. __

trip - per;

It took me

F7   E7   A7

so _____   long   to find out, ___   and I found

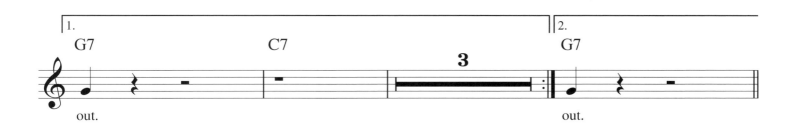

1.
G7   C7   **3**   2.
                                                        G7

out.   out.

Interlude
G7

Guitar Solo
                    G7

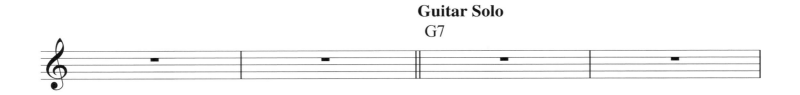

D.S. al Coda

Breakdown
C7

9

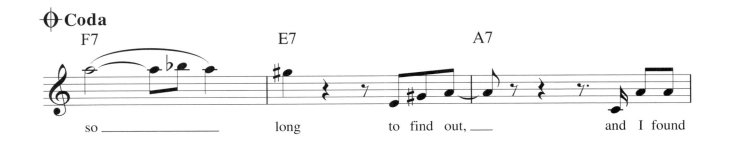

Coda

F7   E7   A7

so _____ long   to find out, ___   and I found

Breakdown

G7   C7

out.

Outro

Play 3 times   C7

Day   trip - per,

day   trip - per,   yeah. ___

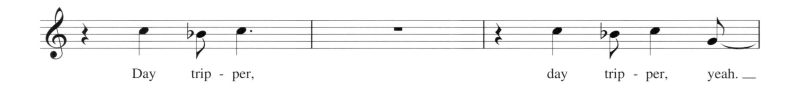

Day   trip - per,   day   trip - per,   yeah. ___

Fade out

___   Day   trip - per.

Good Day Sunshine

Words and Music by John Lennon and Paul McCartney

Intro
Moderately ♩ = 118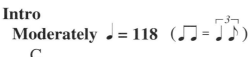

Chorus

Good day __ sun - shine. Good day __ sun - shine.

Good day __ sun - shine. 1. I need to laugh, __ and when the

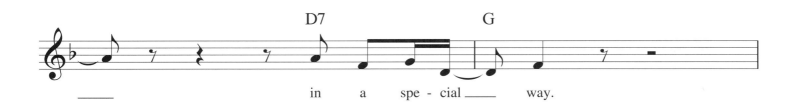

sun is out., __ I've __ got some-thing I can laugh a - bout. I feel good __

__ in a spe - cial __ way.

I'm __ in love, __ an' it's a sun - ny day. __

Chorus

Good day __ sun - shine.   Good day __ sun - shine.

Verse

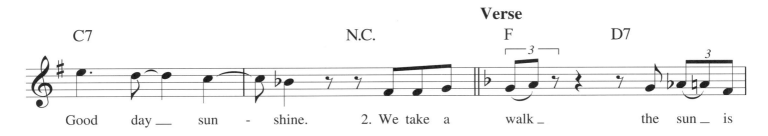

Good day __ sun - shine.   2. We take a   walk __   the sun __ is

shin - ing down,   burns __ my __ feet as they touch __ the ground. ___

Piano solo

Chorus

Good day __ sun - shine.   Good day __ sun - shine.

Verse

Good day __ sun - shine.   3. Then we'd   lie, __   be - neath a

sha - dy tree.   I __ love her and she's lov - ing me.   She feels good. _

She knows she's look-ing fine. ___

I'm so proud to know that she is mine.

Chorus

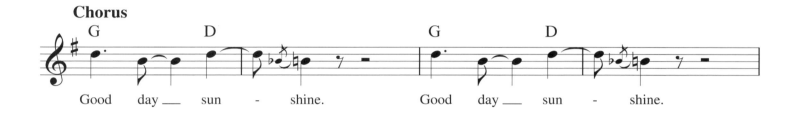

Good day ___ sun - shine. Good day ___ sun - shine.

Good day ___ sun - shine.

Good day ___ sun - shine.

Good day ___ sun - shine.

Repeat & fade

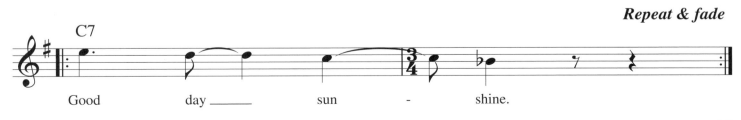

Good day ___ sun - shine.

Eight Days a Week

Words and Music by John Lennon and Paul McCartney

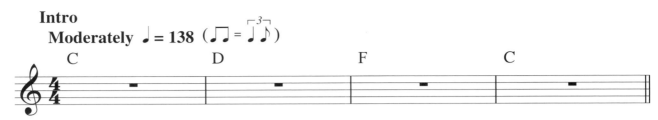

1., 3. Oo, I need your love, babe, ___ guess you know it's true. ___
2., 4. Love you ev - 'ry day, ___ girl, ___ al - ways on my mind. ___

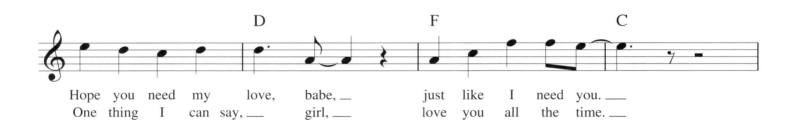

Hope you need my love, babe, ___ just like I need you. ___
One thing I can say, ___ girl, ___ love you all the time. ___

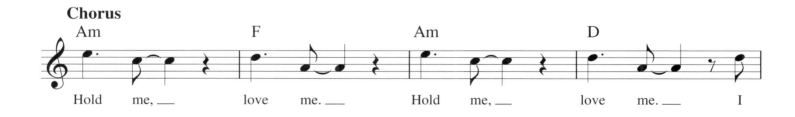

Hold me, ___ love me. ___ Hold me, ___ love me. ___ I

ain't got noth-in' but love, { 1., 3., 4. babe, ___ / 2. girl, ___ } eight days a week. ___

Bridge

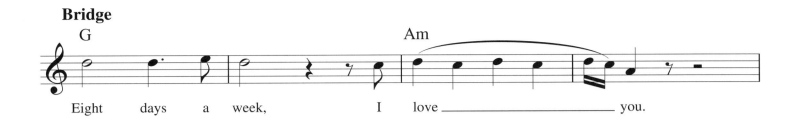

Eight days a week, I love you.

To Coda 1 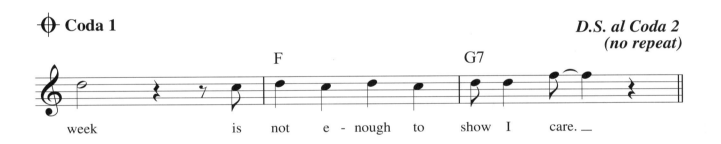 *D.S. al Coda 1 (no repeat)*

Eight days a week is not e-nough to show I care.

Coda 1 *D.S. al Coda 2 (no repeat)*

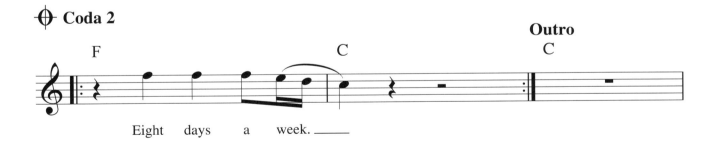

week is not e-nough to show I care.

Coda 2 **Outro**

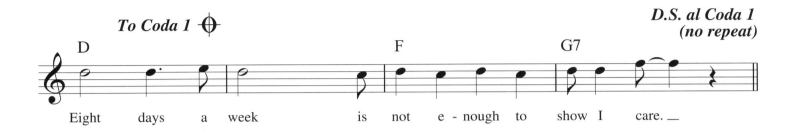

Eight days a week.

Get Back

Words and Music by John Lennon and Paul McCartney

Intro
Moderately ♩ = 123

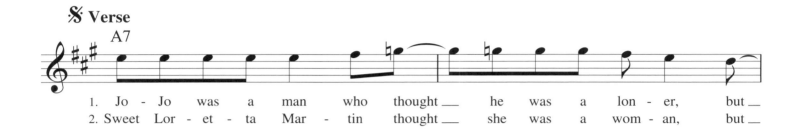

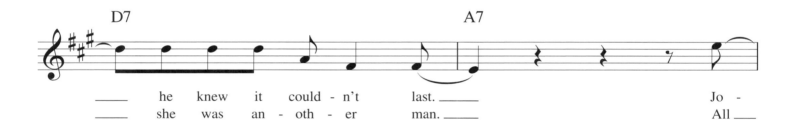

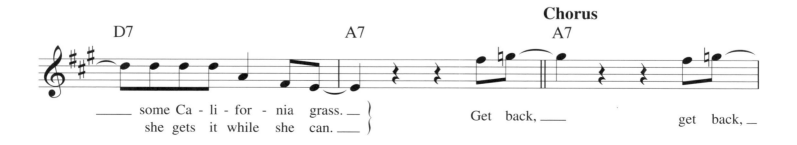

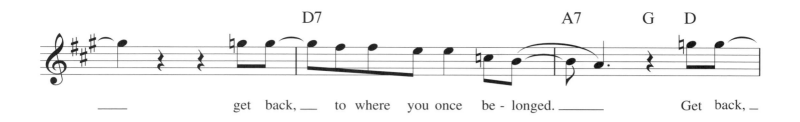

get back, — to where you once be - longed. ——— Get back, —

— get back, — get back — to where you once be - longed. —

To Coda ⊕ **Guitar Solo**

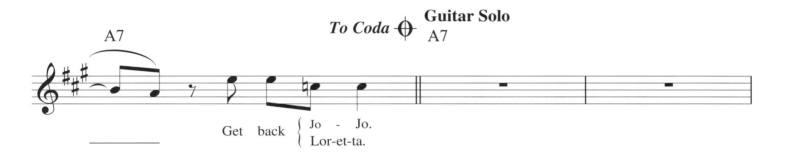

Get back { Jo - Jo. / Lor-et-ta.

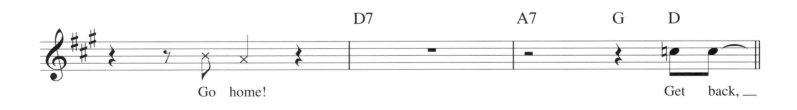

Go home! Get back, —

Chorus

— get back, — back — to where you once be - longed.

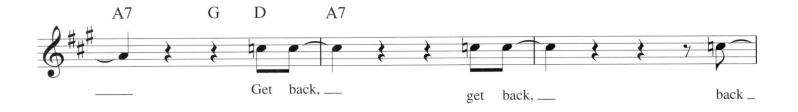

Get back, ___   get back, ___   back ___

___ to where you once be - longed. ___   Here.   Uh, get back Jo!

Piano Solo

D.S. al Coda   **⊕ Coda**
Guitar Solo

A Hard Day's Night

Words and Music by John Lennon and Paul McCartney

Help!

Words and Music by John Lennon and Paul McCartney

Intro

Fast ♩ = 188

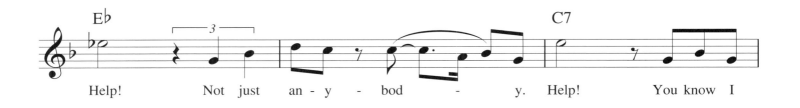

Help! I need some-bod - y.

Help! Not just an - y - bod - y. Help! You know I

need some - one.___ Help!___

Verse

1., 3. When I___ was youn - ger. so___ much
2. And now my life has changed___ in

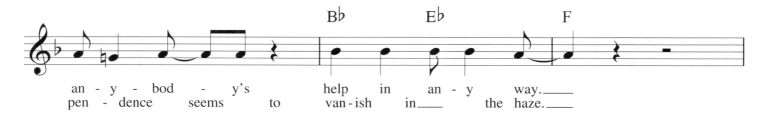

young - ger than___ to - day,___ I nev - er need - ed
oh, so man - y ways.___ My in - de -

an - y - bod - y's help in an - y way.___
pen - dence seems to van - ish in___ the haze.___

Here Comes the Sun

Words and Music by George Harrison

Intro

Moderately ♩ = 126

G | | C | D7

G | | C | D7

Chorus

G ... C

Here comes_ the sun,____ doo 'n' doo, doo. Here comes_ the sun_

A7 ... G ... C G Am G D

____ 'n' I____ say____ it's al - right.

Verse

G ... C ... D7

1. Lit - tle dar - lin', it's_ been_ a__ long,___ cold,_ lone - ly win - ter.

G ... C ... D7

Lit - tle dar - lin', it__ feels_ like_ years_ since it's_ been here.__

Chorus

G ... C

Here comes_ the sun,____ doo 'n' doo, doo. Here_ comes_ the sun_

Bridge

Sun, sun, sun, here it comes._

Sun, sun, sun, here it comes._

D.S. al Coda

Coda

Here comes_ the sun._ Here comes_ the sun._

It's al - right.

It's al - right.

Hey Jude

Words and Music by John Lennon and Paul McCartney

Verse

Slow ♩ = 74

1. Hey Jude don't make it bad, take a sad song__ and make it
   Jude don't be a‑fraid, you were made to__ go out and

bet‑ter.__ Re‑mem‑ber to let her in‑to your
get her.__ The min‑ute you let her un‑der your

heart, then you can start__ to make it__ bet‑ter. 2. Hey
skin, then you be‑gin__ to make it__ bet‑ter.

𝄋 Bridge

And an‑y‑time__ you feel the pain,__ hey Jude__ re‑frain,__
__ hey Jude__ be‑gin,__

__ don't car‑ry the world__ up‑on__ your shoul‑
__ you're wait‑ing for some‑one to__ per‑form__

-der.____ For well, you know___ that it's a fool___
____ with.____ And don't you know___ that it's just you?___

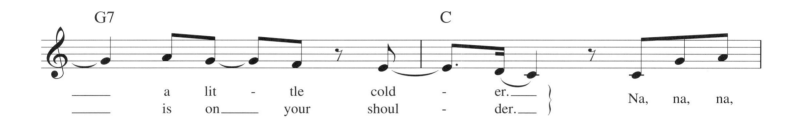

____ who plays___ it cool___ by mak - ing his world___
____ Hey Jude___ you'll do,___ the move - ment you need___

____ a lit - tle cold - er.____ Na, na, na,
____ is on___ your shoul - der.____

To Coda ⊕

na,___ na, na, na, na, na. 3., 4. Hey___

Verse

Jude don't let me down. You have found her, now go and

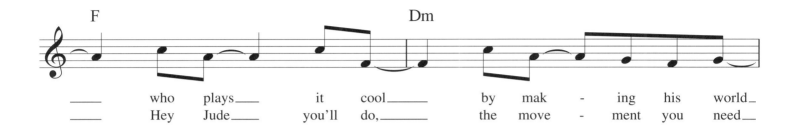

get her.____ Re - mem - ber to let her in - to your

heart, then you can start___ to make it___ bet - ter.

D.S. al Coda

⊕ **Coda**
Verse

So let it out___ and let it in,___ Jude_____ don't make it

bad, take a sad song and make it

bet - ter.___ Re - mem - ber to let her un - der your

skin, then you be - gin_____ to make it bet -

Outro

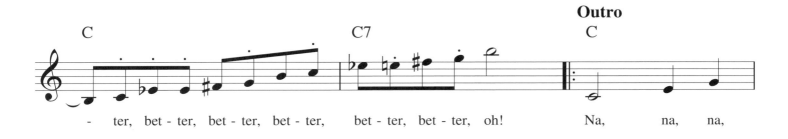

- ter, bet - ter, bet - ter, bet - ter, bet - ter, bet - ter, oh! Na, na, na,

Repeat & fade

na, na, na, na, na, na, na, na, hey___ Jude.

I Feel Fine

Words and Music by John Lennon and Paul McCartney

Intro
Fast ♩ = 180

1. Ba - by's good to me, you know, she's hap -
2., 4. Ba - by says she's mine, you know, she tells

- py as can be, you know, she said so. }
me all the time, you know, she said so. }

I'm in love with her and I feel fine.

Bridge

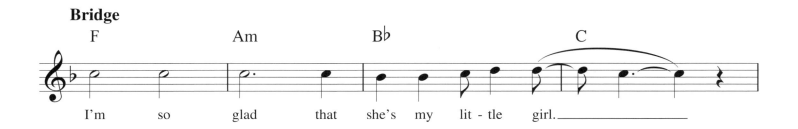

I'm so glad that she's my lit-tle girl._____

She's so glad, she's tell-in' all___ the world___ 3. that her ba-

Verse

- by buys her things,___ you know,___ he buys___

___ her dia-mond rings,___ you know,___ she said___ so.

To Coda ✈

She's in love with me___ and I___ feel___ fine. Mm._____

D.S. al Coda
(no repeat)

Coda

fine.   She's   in   love   with   me___

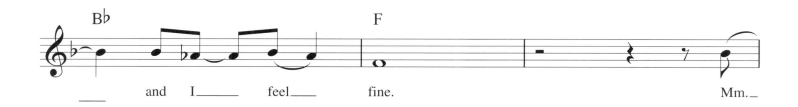

___   and   I___   feel___   fine.   Mm.___

Begin fade   *Fade out*

Revolution

Words and Music by John Lennon and Paul McCartney

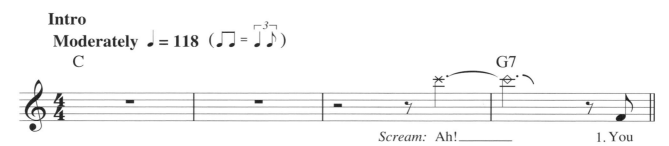

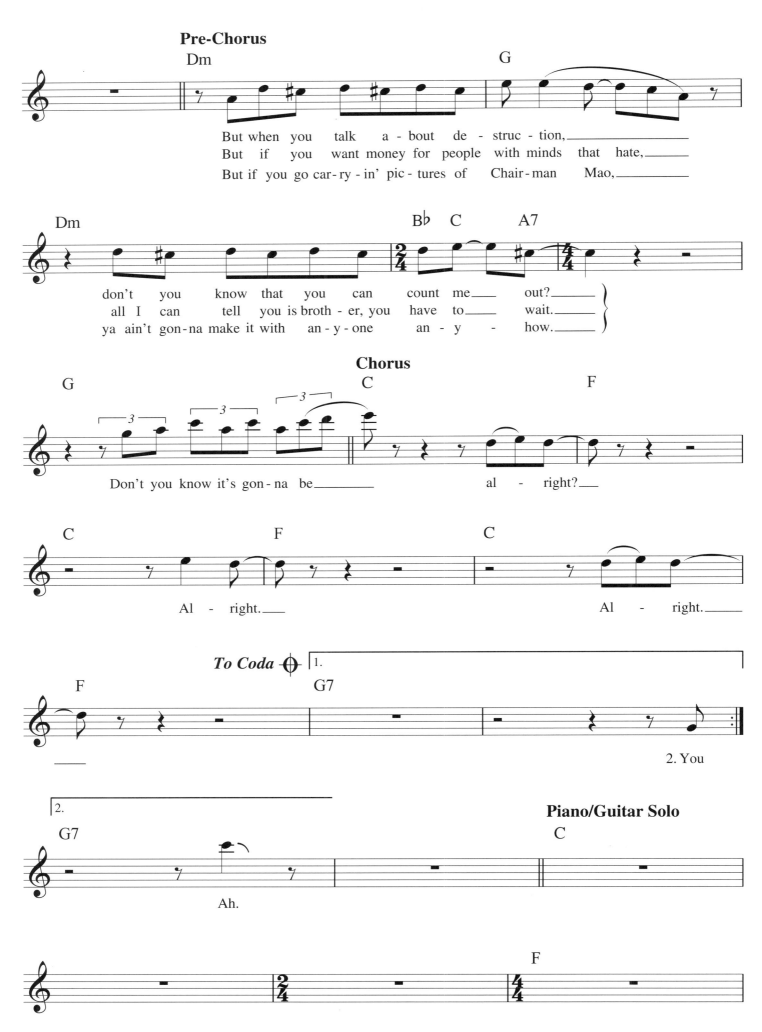

G7

D.S. al Coda

3. You

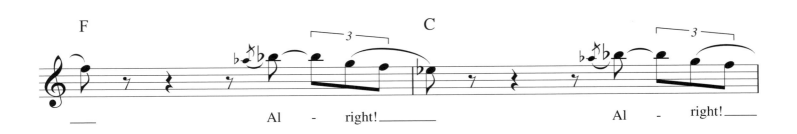

⊕ **Coda**

Outro-Chorus

G7   C

Al - right!___   Al - right!___

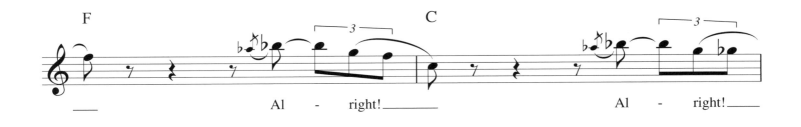

F   C

___   Al - right!___   Al - right!___

F   C

___   Al - right!___   Al - right!___

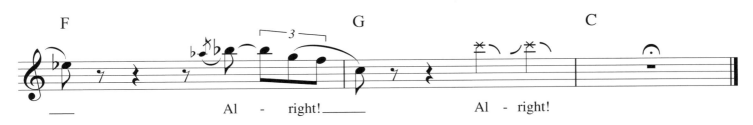

F   G   C

___   Al - right!___   Al - right!

I Saw Her Standing There

Words and Music by John Lennon and Paul McCartney

Intro
Fast ♩ = 160

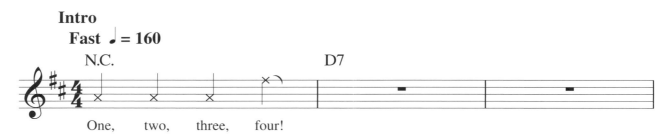

One, two, three, four!

Verse

1. Well, she was just___ sev - en - teen,___

___ if you know what I___ mean.___ And the

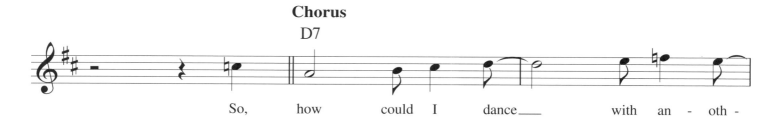

way she looked was way be - yond com - pare.___

Chorus

So, how could I dance___ with an - oth -

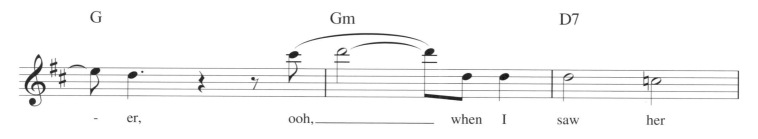

- er, ooh,___ when I saw her

crossed   that   room____   and   I   held   her   hand__

____   in   mine._____

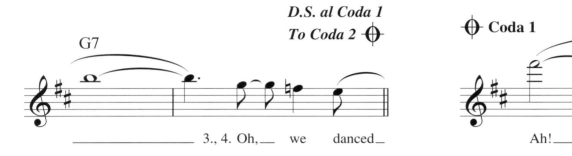

D.S. al Coda 1
To Coda 2 ⊕

⊕ Coda 1

_____ 3., 4. Oh,___ we   danced__

Ah!_____

Guitar Solo

D.S.S. al Coda 2

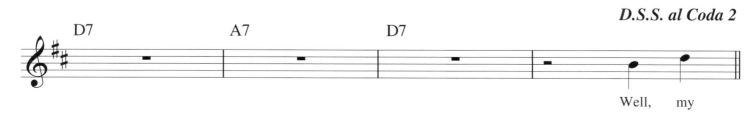

Well,   my

Coda 2
Verse

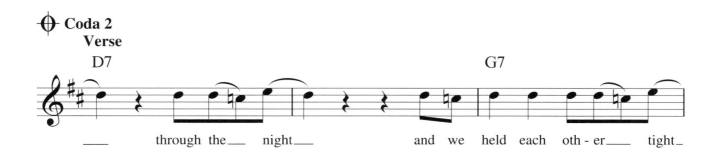

through the ___ night ___ and we held each oth-er ___ tight ___

___ and be - fore too long I ___

___ fell in love ___ with her. ___ Now,

Outro-Chorus

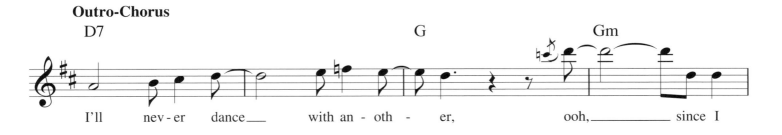

I'll nev-er dance ___ with an-oth - er, ooh, ___ since I

saw her stand - ing there. ___ Oh, since I

saw her stand - ing there. ___ Yeah, well, since I

saw her stand - ing there. ___

Let It Be

Words and Music by John Lennon and Paul McCartney

Intro
Slow ♩ = 73

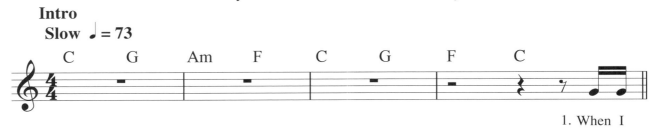

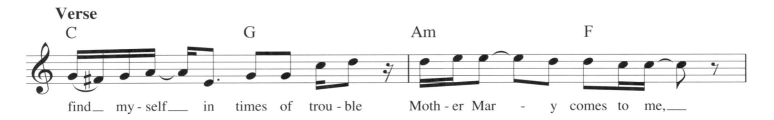

1. When I

Verse

find__ my-self__ in times of trou - ble Moth - er Mar - y comes to me,__

speak - ing words of wis - dom, let it be.__ And

in my hour of dark - ness she is stand - ing right in front of me,

speak - ing words of wis - dom, let it be.__ Let it be,__

Chorus

__ let it be. Ah, let it be,_____ let it be.__

Whis - per words of wis - dom, let it be.__ 2. And

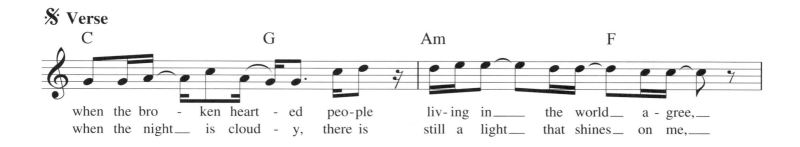

when the bro - ken heart - ed peo-ple liv-ing in____ the world____ a - gree,____
when the night____ is cloud - y, there is still a light____ that shines____ on me,____

there will be an an - swer, let it be.____ For
shine un - til to - mor - row, let it be.____ I

though they may____ be part - ed, there is still a chance____ that they____ will see.____
wake up to____ the sound of mu - sic, Moth-er Mar - y comes to me,____

To Coda ⊕

There will be an an - swer, let it be.____ }
speak - ing words of wis - dom, let it be.____ } Let it be,____

Chorus

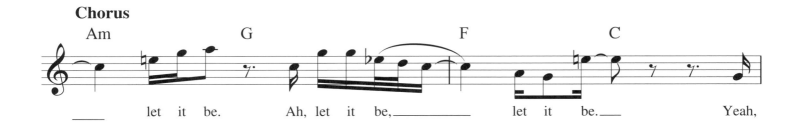

____ let it be. Ah, let it be,_____ let it be.____ Yeah,

there will be an an - swer let it be.____ Let it

be,   let it be.   Ah, let it be,_____   let it be.__

Whis - per words__ of wis - dom,   let it be.____

Interlude

Guitar Solo

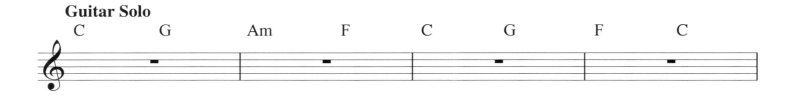

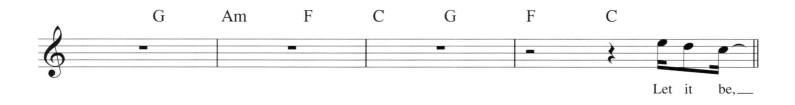

Let it be,__

Chorus

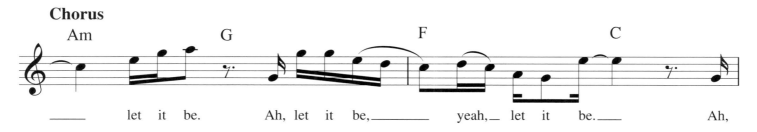

____ let it be.   Ah, let it be,_____ yeah,__ let it be.__   Ah,

whis - per words__ of wis - dom, let it be._____ 3. And

Coda
Chorus

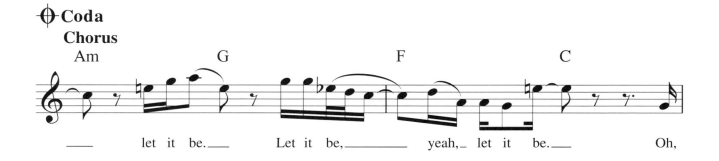

__ let it be.__ Let it be,_____ yeah,_ let it be.__ Oh,

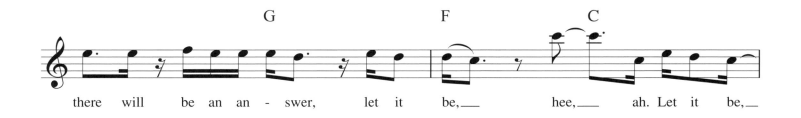

there will be an an - swer, let it be,___ hee,___ ah. Let it be,___

__ let it be. Ah, let it be,_____ yeah, let it be.__

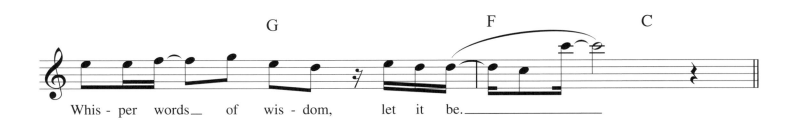

Whis - per words__ of wis - dom, let it be._____

Outro

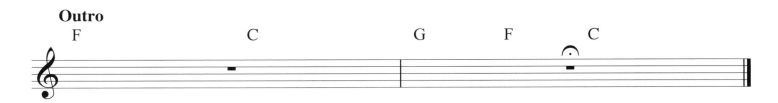

Love Me Do

Words and Music by John Lennon and Paul McCartney

Intro
Moderately fast ♩ = 148

Verse

1.-4. Love, love me do, ___ you know I love you. ___ I'll

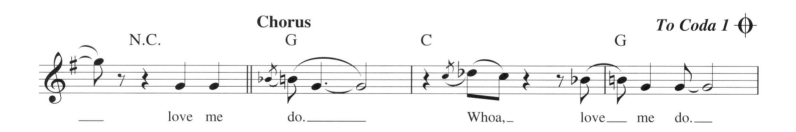

al - ways be true, ___ so ___ please ___

To Coda 2

Chorus   *To Coda 1*

___ love me do. ___ Whoa, ___ love ___ me do. ___

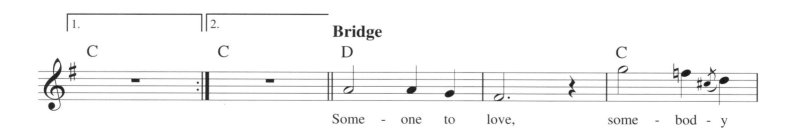

Bridge

Some - one to love, some - bod - y

new._____ Some - one to love, some - one like_ you.

Coda 1

Harmonica Solo

Coda 2

Chorus

____ love me do._____ Whoa,_____ love_

Begin fade

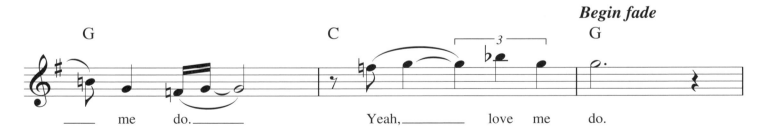

____ me do.___ Yeah,_____ love me do.

Fade out

Whoa,___ love me do._____ Yeah._

Paperback Writer

Words and Music by John Lennon and Paul McCartney

Intro
Moderately fast ♩ = 156

Pa - per - back writ - er,_____

1. Dear
3. It's a

Verse

Sir or Mad - am will you read my book? It took me
Thou - sand pa - ges, give or take a few;___ I'll be

years to write,_ will you take a look? It's based on a nov - el by a
writ - ing more___ in a week or two. I can make it long - er if you like

man named Lear. And I need a job,___ so I } want to be a pa - per - back
the style.___ I can change it 'round, and I }

Chorus

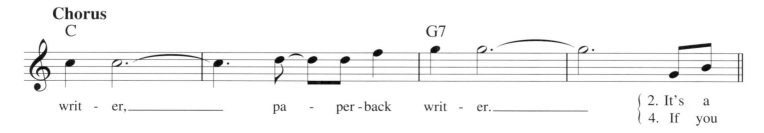

writ - er,_____ pa - per - back writ - er._____

{ 2. It's a
{ 4. If you

Verse

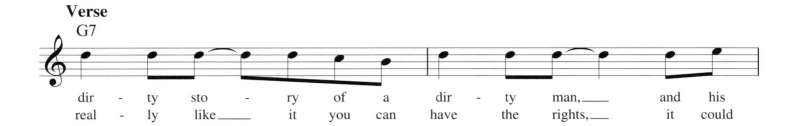

dir - ty sto - ry of a dir - ty man,___ and his
real - ly like___ it you can have the rights,___ it could

cling - ing wife___ does - n't un - der - stand. His son is work - ing for the
make a mil - lion for you o - ver - night. If you must re - turn___ it you can

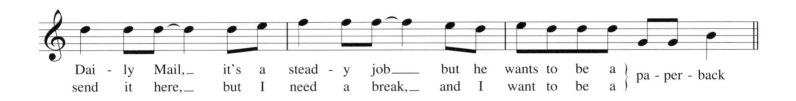

Dai - ly Mail, it's a stead - y job___ but he wants to be a } pa - per - back
send it here,___ but I need a break,___ and I want to be a } pa - per - back

Chorus

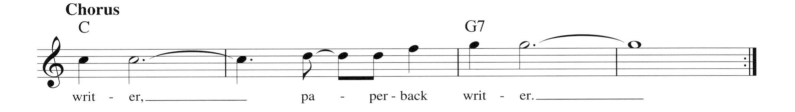

writ - er,_____ pa - per - back writ - er._____

Bridge

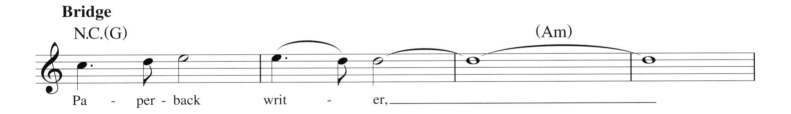

Pa - per - back writ - er,_____

Breakdown

Play 4 times and fade

Outro-Chorus

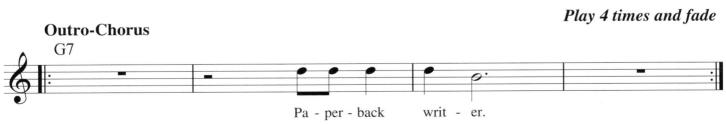

Pa - per - back writ - er.

Twist and Shout

Words and Music by Bert Russell and Phil Medley

Intro
Moderately ♩ = 127

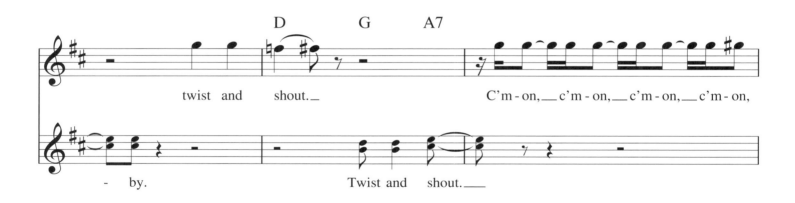

Well, shake it up, ba - by,___ now,___

(Shake it up, ba -

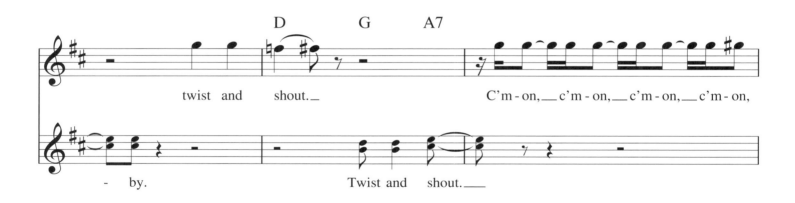

twist and shout.___

C'm-on,___ c'm-on,___ c'm-on,___ c'm-on,

- by.

Twist and shout.___

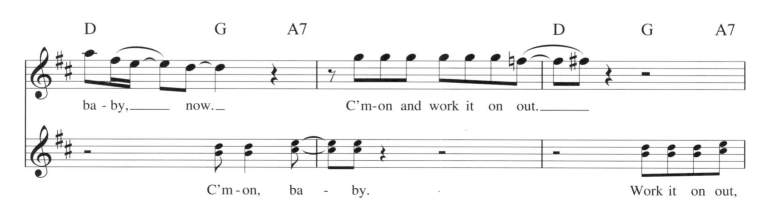

ba - by,___ now.___

C'm-on and work it on out.___

C'm-on, ba - by.

Work it on out,

Bridge

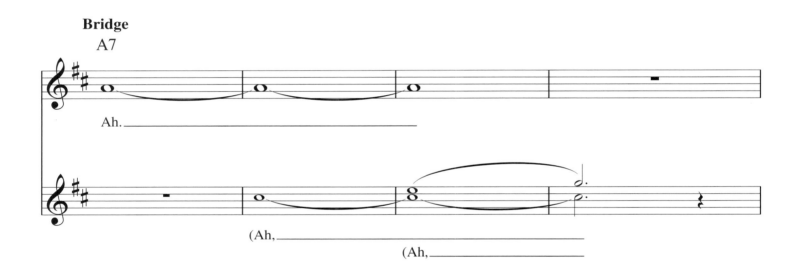

Ah.

(Ah,

(Ah,

D.S. al Coda

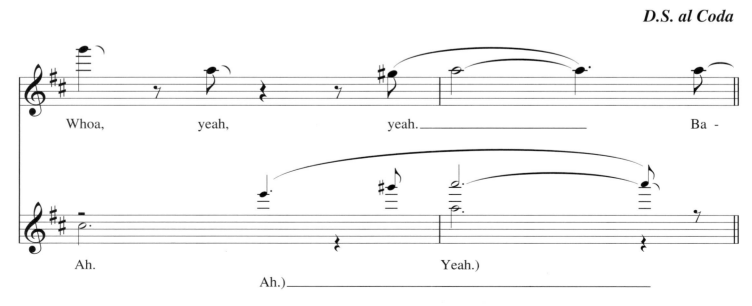

Whoa, yeah, yeah. Ba -

Ah. Yeah.)

Ah.)

Coda

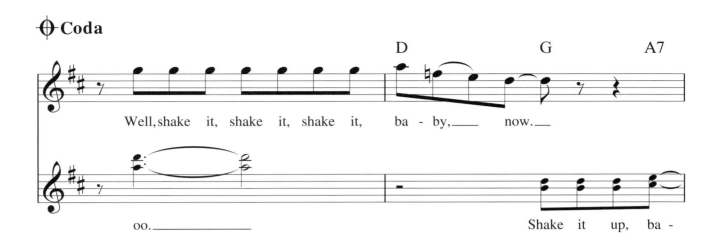

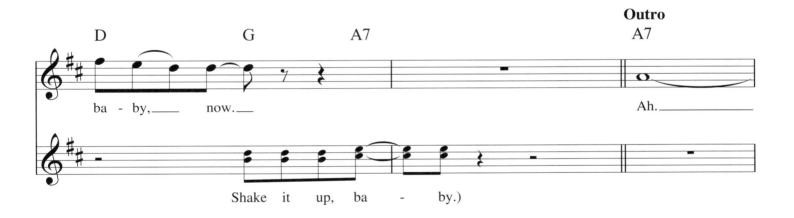

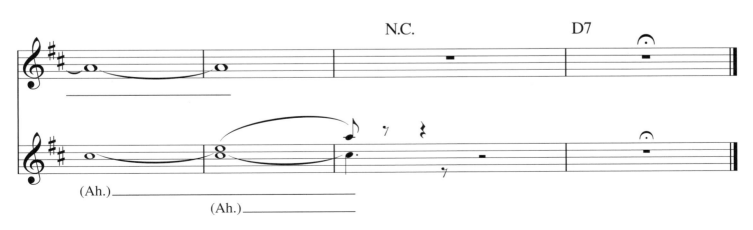

We Can Work It Out

Words and Music by John Lennon and Paul McCartney

Chorus

We can work it out. We can work it out.

Bridge

Life is ver - y short and there's no time

for fuss - ing and fight - ing my friend.

I have al - ways thought that it's a crime,

so I will ask you once a -

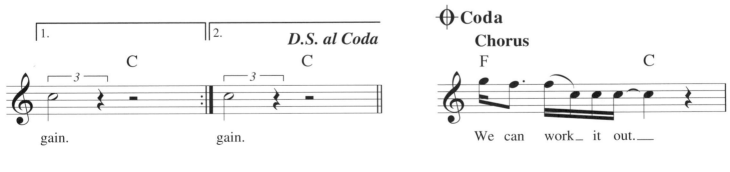

1. gain. 2. gain.

D.S. al Coda

⊕ Coda

Chorus

We can work it out.

We can work it out.

Yellow Submarine

Words and Music by John Lennon and Paul McCartney

You've Got to Hide Your Love Away

Words and Music by John Lennon and Paul McCartney

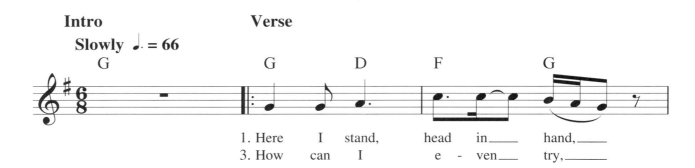

Intro

Verse

Slowly ♩. = 66

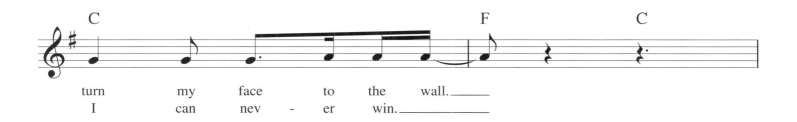

1. Here I stand, head in hand,
3. How can I e- ven try,

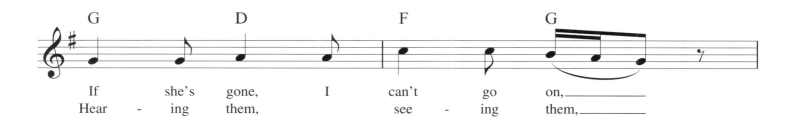

turn my face to the wall.
I can nev - er win.

If she's gone, I can't go on,
Hear - ing them, see - ing them,

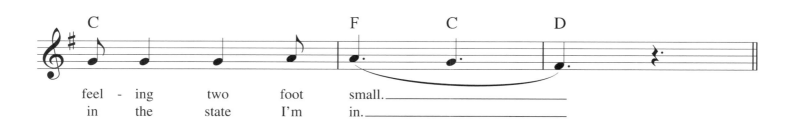

feel - ing two foot small.
in the state I'm in.

Verse

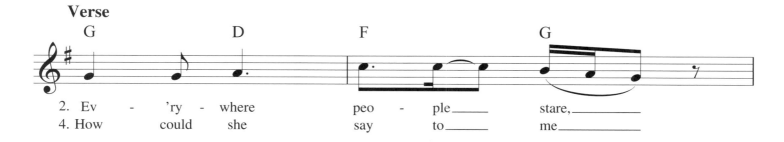

2. Ev - 'ry - where peo - ple stare,
4. How could she say to me

each and_____ ev - 'ry - day._____   I   can   see   them

love will_____ find   a   way?___   Gath - er 'round

laugh   at____ me,_____   and   I_____ hear them   say:_____

all   you____ clowns,___   let   me_____ hear you   say:_____

Chorus

Hey!____   You've   got   to

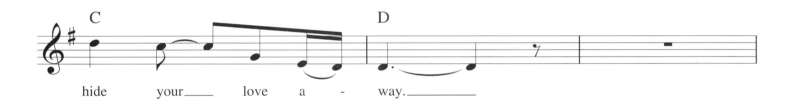

hide   your____ love   a   -   way._____

Hey!____   You've got   to   hide   your____ love   a   -   way._____

Outro

With a Little Help My Friends

Words and Music by John Lennon and Paul McCartney

Verse
Moderately ♩ = 110

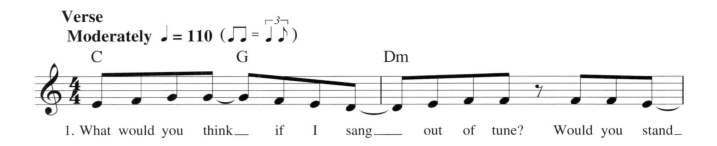

1. What would you think___ if I sang___ out of tune? Would you stand___

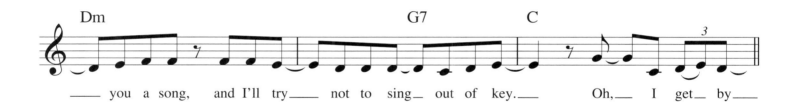

___ up and walk___ out on me?___ Lend me your ears___ and I'll sing___

___ you a song, and I'll try___ not to sing___ out of key.___ Oh,___ I get___ by

Chorus

___ with a lit - tle help from my friends.___ Mmm,___ I get high

___ with a lit - tle help from my friends.___ Mmm,___ gon - na try___

with a lit - tle help   from   my   friends.___

Verse

2. What   do   I   do___   when   my   love___   is   a - way?___

(Does   it   wor -

- y   you   to   be   a - lone?)___

How   do   I   feel___   by   the   end___

___   of   the   day?___

(Are you sad___ be - cause you're on   your own?)___

No,___   I   get   by___

Chorus

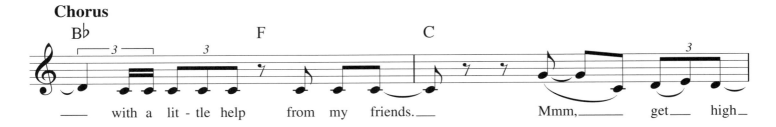

___   with a lit - tle help   from   my   friends.___

Mmm,___   get___   high___

___   with a lit - tle help   from   my   friends.___

Mmm,___   gon - na   try___

with a lit - tle help from my friends.___

(Do you need___

Bridge

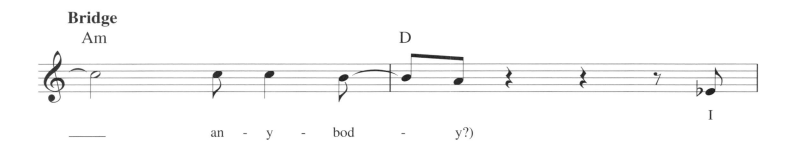

___ an - y - bod - y?)

I

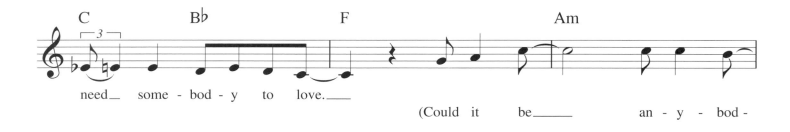

need___ some - bod - y to love.___

(Could it be___ an - y - bod -

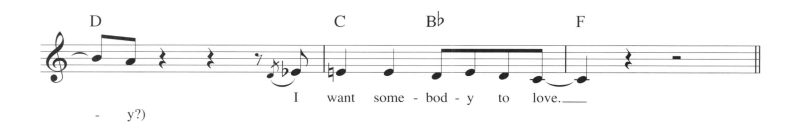

- y?)

I want some - bod - y to love.___

Verse

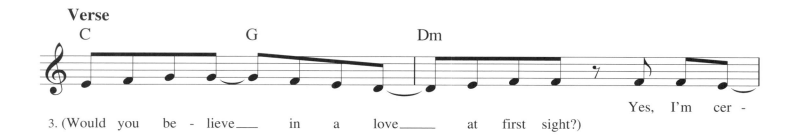

Yes, I'm cer -

3. (Would you be - lieve___ in a love___ at first sight?)

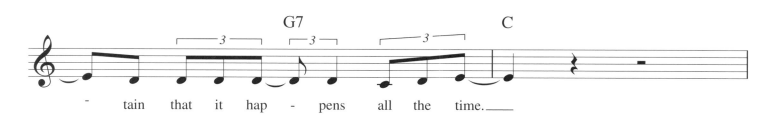

- tain that it hap - pens all the time.___

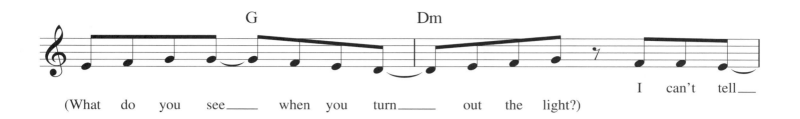

G   Dm

(What do you see___ when you turn___ out the light?)   I can't tell___

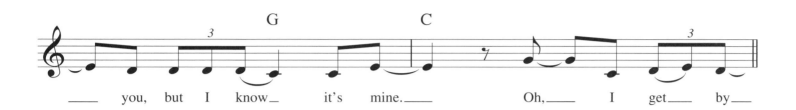

G   C

___ you, but I know___ it's mine.___   Oh,___ I get___ by___

Chorus

B♭   F   C

___ with a lit - tle help from my friends.___   Mmm,___ get___ high___

B♭   F   C

___ with a lit - tle help from my friends.___   Oh,___ I'm gon - na try___

F   C

___ with a lit - tle help from my friends.___   (Do you need___

Bridge

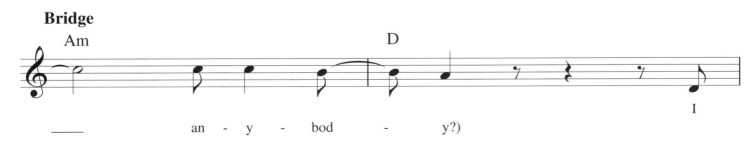

Am   D

___ an - y - bod - y?)   I

Chorus

Learn To Play Today
with folk music instruction from

 **Hal Leonard Banjo Method –
Second Edition**

Authored by Mac Robertson, Robbie Clement & Will Schmid. This innovative method teaches 5-string, bluegrass style. The method consists of two instruction books and two cross-referenced supplement books that offer the beginner a carefully-paced and interest-keeping approach to the bluegrass style.

Method Book 1
00699500 Book $6.95
00695101 Book/CD Pack $16.95

Method Book 2
00699502 .... $6.95

Supplementary Songbooks
00699515 Easy Banjo Solos $7.99
00699516 More Easy Banjo Solos $7.99

 **Hal Leonard Dulcimer Method –
Second Edition**

by Neal Hellman

A beginning method for the Appalachian dulcimer with a unique new approach to solo melody and chord playing. Includes tuning, modes and many beautiful folk songs all demonstrated on the audio accompaniment. Music and tablature.
00699289 Book $7.99
00697230 Book/CD Pack $16.99

 **The Hal Leonard Complete
Harmonica Method –
Chromatic Harmonica**

by Bobby Joe Holman

The only harmonica method to present the chromatic harmonica in 14 scales and modes in all 12 keys!
00841286 Book/CD Pack $12.95

 **The Hal Leonard Complete
Harmonica Method –
The Diatonic Harmonica**

by Bobby Joe Holman

This terrific method book/CD pack specific to the diatonic harmonica covers all six positions! It contains more than 20 songs and musical examples.
00841285 Book/CD Pack $12.95

 **Hal Leonard Fiddle Method**

by Chris Wagoner

The Hal Leonard Fiddle Method is the perfect introduction to playing folk, bluegrass and country styles on the violin. Many traditional tunes are included to illustrate a variety of techniques. The accompanying CD includes many tracks for demonstration and play-along. Covers: instrument selection and care; playing positions; theory; slides & slurs; shuffle feel; bowing; drones; playing "backup"; cross-tuning; and much more!
00311415 Book $5.99
00311416 Book/CD Pack $9.99

 **The Hal Leonard Mandolin
Method – Second Edition**

Noted mandolinist and teacher Rich Del Grosso has authored this excellent mandolin method that features great playable tunes in several styles (bluegrass, country, folk, blues) in standard music notation and tablature. The audio features play-along duets.
00699296 Book $7.99
00695102 Book/CD Pack $15.99

 **Hal Leonard Oud Method**

by John Bilezikjian

This book teaches the fundamentals of standard Western music notation in the context of oud playing. It also covers: types of ouds, tuning the oud, playing position, how to string the oud, scales, chords, arpeggios, tremolo technique, studies and exercises, songs and rhythms from Armenia and the Middle East, and a CD with 25 tracks for demonstration and play along.
00695836 Book/CD Pack $10.99

 **Hal Leonard Ukulele Method
Book 1**

INCLUDES TAB

by Lil' Rev

This comprehensive and easy-to-use beginner's guide by acclaimed performer and uke master Lil' Rev includes many fun songs of different styles to learn and play. Includes: types of ukuleles, tuning, music reading, melody playing, chords, strumming, scales, tremolo, music notation and tablature, a variety of music styles, ukulele history and much more.
00695847 Book $5.95
00695832 Book/CD Pack $10.99

FOR MORE INFORMATION, SEE YOUR LOCAL MUSIC DEALER,
OR WRITE TO:

7777 W. BLUEMOUND RD. P.O. BOX 13819 MILWAUKEE, WI 53213

Visit Hal Leonard Online at
www.halleonard.com

Prices and availability subject to change without notice.